MW00721414

PRAYERS

for

Mealtime

DIMENSIONS

FOR LIVING

NASHVILLE

EVERYDAY PRAYERS FOR MEALTIME

Copyright © 1994 by Dimensions for Living

All rights reserved.
No part of this work may be reproduced or transmitted in any form or by any means, electronic or mechanical, including photocopying and recording, or by any information storage or retrieval system, except as may be expressly permitted by the 1976 Copyright Act or in writing from the publisher. Requests for permission should be addressed in writing to Dimensions for Living, P.O. Box 801, 201 Eighth Avenue South, Nashville, TN 37202.

This book is printed on recycled, acid-free paper.

0-687-00320-2

Prayers on pages 5-10, 16-19, 21-27, 45, 48, 50, 52, 54, 56, 61, 63, 65, 67, 69, 71, 73, 75, and 77 are paraphrased from *Table Graces For All Ages* by Gertrude duBois, copyright © 1952 by Pierce and Washabaugh.

Scripture quotations are pharaphrased.

94 95 96 97 98 99 00 01 02 03 — 10 9 8 7 6 5 4 3 2 1

MANUFACTURED IN THE UNITED STATES OF AMERICA

Contents

Morning Graces

In the morning we turn our thoughts to you, O Lord; help us always to remember that all our blessings throughout the day come from you. Amen.

Our Father, you are nearer to us than our breathing through all the hours of the day. Help us to live by the strength you give us. Amen.

We lay down and slept. We awakened, for you, O Lord, sustained us. May your grace be sufficient for the hours of the day before us. Through Christ we pray. Amen.

Your presence is near in the morning
and never leaves us throughout the day.
We give you our thanks for all, O Lord.
Amen.

As the morning stars sing together in your praise, we lift our hearts to you at the beginning of this new day. We ask you to stay close beside us all day. Through Christ our Lord. Amen.

"In the morning you shall see the glory of the Lord." We thank you, dear God, for your great glory. May it be upon us today. Amen.

(Exodus 16:7)

Let our prayer, O Lord, come before Thee in the morning. Thou didst take upon Thee our feeble and suffering nature; grant us to pass this day in gladness and peace, without stumbling and without stain; that reaching the eventide free from evil, we may praise Thee, the eternal King: through Thy mercy, O our God, Who art blessed, and dost live, and govern all things, world without end.

St. Anselm
Eleventh Century

Lord, give us to go blithely on our business all this day, bring us to our resting beds weary and content and undishonoured, and grant us in the end the gift of sleep.

Robert Louis Stevenson

O God, who hast folded back the mantle of the night, to clothe us in the golden glory of the day, chase from our hearts all gloomy thoughts, and make us glad with the brightness of hope, that we may effectively aspire to unwon virtues; through Jesus Christ our Lord.

Ancient Collect
A.D. *590*

O Lord, thou knowest how busy I must
be this day; if I forget thee, do not thou
forget me; for Christ's sake.

General Lord Astley
1579–1652
(before the battle of Edgehill)

Make me remember, O God, that every day is your gift and ought to be used according to thy command, through Jesus Christ our Lord.

Samuel Johnson
1709–1786

Evening Graces

Stay with us now, O Lord, for the day is nearly over. Be our guest as the evening shadows fall. Amen.

As the peace of evening steals over the earth, so may your peace come into our hearts as we gather here. Through Christ our Lord. Amen.

We thank you for the gentle darkness, dear Lord, knowing that darkness and light are both alike to you. May the shadow of your wings be over us till morning dawns. Amen.

O God, our Maker, you give songs in the night; grant us now your evening blessing. Through Christ our Lord. Amen.

Watch thou, dear Lord, with those who wake and watch or weep tonight, and give thine angels charge over those who sleep. Tend thy sick ones, O Lord Christ; rest thy weary ones; bless thy dying ones; soothe thy suffering ones; shield thy joyous ones; and all for thy Love's sake.

St. Augustine
354–430

Children's Graces

I must always, say "thank you,"
   When someone is kind and good;
So dear Lord, I now say, thank you
   For my daily food. Amen.

Dear Lord, you know I need food
    To keep me strong and sweet and good,
And I will try my thanks to say
    By loving you all through the day. Amen.

Father, we thank thee for the night
And for the pleasant morning light,
For rest and food and loving care,
And all that makes the day so fair.

Help us to do the things we should,
To be to others kind and good,
In all we do in work or play
To grow more loving every day. Amen.

Rebecca Weston, 1885

My parents tell me to count my blessings
    So I count them up to ten,
But after that there are so many
    I begin again.
Thank you, our Father in heaven. Amen.

All the little children praise you
> For your care and tender love,
For our food and for our houses,
> For the sun that shines above. Amen.

Bless us, Jesus, in our home;
    Bless all those across the sea,
Please send needed food and drink
    Everyday for them and me. Amen.

Thank you, Lord, for loving me.
  Help me now to be
Very happy all the day
  For all you give to me. Amen.

Good morning, God. Thank you for my food. Help me to be loving and helpful all day. Amen.

Can a growing child like me
thank the Father fittingly?
Yes, O yes, be good and true,
Patient, kind in all you do;
Love the Lord and do your part,
Learn to say with all your heart,
Father, we thank thee,
Father, we thank thee,
Father in heaven,
we thank Thee.

For the fruit upon the tree,
For the birds that sing of Thee,
For the earth in beauty dressed,
Father, mother, and the rest,
For thy precious, loving care,
For Thy bounty everywhere,
Father we thank thee,
Father we thank thee,
Father in heaven,
We thank thee.

Attributed to Mary Mapes Dodge
1831—1905

A Breakfast Prayer

Lord, we are grateful for this new day you have given us. Wherever the day may take us and whatever the day may hold, may we remember that you go with us. Amen.

A Lunch Prayer

Dear Lord, as we take a break from the day's activities and enjoy the good food you have provided, we ask that you replenish our minds and bodies and prepare us for the rest of the day. Amen.

Dinner Prayer

O God, we know you watch over us, for we have felt your loving presence throughout the day—protecting, guiding, and sustaining us. For your constant care and the blessings of this day, we offer our gratitude and praise. Amen.

For a Birthday

Be with us, O Lord, as we share this meal from your bounty and recall with joy the day _____ was born. You have filled our lives with your blessings. We will praise you forever. Amen.

On a Picnic

Dear God, we are happy to be here today.

It is good to share this food in a place where we can smell grass, trees, and flowers.

It is good to share this food in a place where we can touch the earth and feel the warmth of the sun.

It is good to share this food in a place where we can hear birds singing.

It is good to share this food in a place where we can see the wonders of your creation.

Amen.

A New Year's Prayer

Lord, the promise of a new year is before us, and we are thankful for the opportunities it holds for our family. Bless this food to the nourishment of our bodies, so that we may begin the year with strength to serve you in all we do. Amen.

A Valentine's Day Prayer

Lord, today we celebrate love and give thanks for loved ones around this table and others we hold dear in our hearts. We thank you for the food and the love we share. Amen.

An Easter Prayer

Heavenly Father, you loved us so much that you gave your only Son so that we might have eternal life. Today as we gather around this table, we celebrate the new life we have through him and praise you with joyful hearts, knowing that Christ has conquered sin and death. May the joy of Easter be with us each and every day. Amen.

A Mother's Day Prayer

A mother is a special blessing to her family, Lord, and we are grateful that you have blessed our family so richly. Today we say thank you for a very special mother. As we share this meal together, may we also share our love and laughter. Amen.

A Father's Day Prayer

Heavenly Father, we know that you love us as a father loves his children. Thank you for loving fathers who show their children just how much they are loved—especially the one(s) sitting at this table. In Jesus' name. Amen.

A Fourth of July Prayer

Dear God, today we are grateful for the opportunity to share food, fun, and fellowship as we celebrate our nation's independence. Pour out your blessings upon this food and those gathered here, and help us to appreciate the freedoms we so often take for granted. In Jesus' name. Amen.

A Labor Day Prayer

May the work of our hands and the fruits of our labor be pleasing to you, O Lord. Amen.

A Thanksgiving Prayer

Gracious God, you are the giver of all
things. Today we give special thanks for all
the gifts you have given us—gifts we often
take for granted. Today we celebrate the
gifts of family, friends, love, and life and
say "thank you" for the many ways you
have blessed us.

[Each person says a sentence prayer,
beginning "Thank you, God, for . . ."]

For all these things, and the meal before
us, we give you thanks, O God. Help us
always to have grateful hearts. We pray in
Jesus' name—your greatest gift of all.
Amen.

A Christmas Prayer

O God, as we celebrate the birth of your Son, Jesus Christ, we are grateful for the opportunity to share this special meal together. Fill our hearts with joy and peace, and help us to remember today and every day that the most precious gift of all is love. Amen.

Christmas Day

Moonless darkness stands between.
Past, O Past, no more be seen!
But the Bethlehem star may lead me
To the sight of Him who freed me
From the self that I have been.
Make me pure, Lord: Thou art holy;
Make me meek, Lord: Thou wert lowly;
Now beginning, and alway:
Now begin, on Christmas Day.

Gerard Manley Hopkins
1844–1889

General Graces

Our gracious Lord, thank you for the tree which brings forth fruit in season, for ripening grain, for meat which gives us strength. Help us to always be mindful of your love which planned all things for your children. Amen.

Lord, as we enjoy your gifts of food and drink, give us gratitude, wisdom, and generosity. In everything we do, including our eating and drinking, help us to give glory to you. Amen.

Savior, no offering
Costly and sweet,
May we, like Magdalene,
Lay at Thy feet;
Yet may love's incense rise,
Sweeter than sacrifice,
Dear Lord, to Thee,
O gracious Lord, to Thee.

Some word of hope for hearts
Burdened with fears,
Some balm of peace, for eyes
Blinded with tears;
Some dews of mercy shed,
Some wayward footsteps led,
Dear Lord, to Thee,
O gracious Lord, to Thee.

Edwin P. Parker, 1888

To you who fills the hungry with good things and satisfies the desire of every living thing, we return our thanks, through Jesus Christ. Amen.

Now thank we all our God,
with heart and hands and voices,
who wondrous things has done,
in whom this world rejoices;
who from our mothers' arms
has blessed us on our way
with countless gifts of love,
and still is ours today.

O may this bounteous God
through all our life be near us,
with ever joyful hearts
and blessed peace to cheer us;
and keep us still in grace,
and guide us when perplexed;
and free us from all ills,
in this world and the next.

Martin Rinkart, 1663
Translation by Catherine Winkworth, 1858

Your benefits, O Lord, who can forget! Who can keep silence concerning your mercies! May the flame of thankful remembrance warm our hearts each day, we pray. Amen.

I sing the almighty power of God,
That made the mountains rise,
That spread the flowing seas abroad,
And built the lofty skies.

I sing the goodness of the Lord,
that filled the earth with food,
And formed the creatures with His
    word,
And then pronounced them good.

Lord, how thy wonders are displayed
Where'er I turn mine eyes,
There's not a place where we can flee,
But Thou, O God, art nigh.

Isaac Watts, 1715

Put new vigor into our thankfulness, our Father. May the remembrance of your merciful dealings with us strengthen our praise. Amen.

All things bright and beautiful
All things great and small,
All things wise and wonderful,
Our Father made them all.
Each little flower that opens,
Each little bird that sings,
He made their glowing colors,
He made their tiny wings.

Cold wind in the winter,
Pleasant summer sun,
Ripe fruits in the garden,
He made them, every one.
He gave us eyes to see them,
And lips that we might tell
How good is God our Father,
Who doeth all things well.

Cecil F. Alexander, 1848

The heavens are the heavens of Jehovah, but the earth you gave to us. Teach us the right use of this your gift, so that no child shall want bread. Amen.

Sing to the Lord of the harvest,
Sing songs of love and praise;
With joyful hearts and voices
Your alleluias raise;
By Him the rolling seasons
In fruitful order move;
Sing to the Lord of the harvest
A song of happy love.

By Him the clouds drop fatness,
The deserts bloom and spring,
The hills leap up in gladness,
The valleys laugh and sing,
He filleth with His fullness
All things with large increase;
He crowns the year with goodness,
With plenty and with peace.

J. S. B. Monsell, 1866

O Tender Shepherd, you lead us in green pastures by gently flowing streams. By your mercy help us to feed your lambs and offer cooling drinks to the sheep of your flock. Through Jesus Christ. Amen.

Let us with a gladsome mind
Praise the Lord, for he is kind;
For his mercies aye endure,
Ever faithful, ever sure.

He, with all commanding might,
Filled the new-made world with light;
For his mercies aye endure,
Ever faithful, ever sure.

All things living he doth feed;
His full hand supplies their need;
For his mercies aye endure,
Ever faithful, ever sure.

Let us with a gladsome mind
Praise the Lord, for he is kind;
For his mercies aye endure,
Ever faithful, ever sure.

John Milton, 1624

You have never allowed your faithfulness to fail, our Father, nor taken your loving-kindness from us. Bind us strongly to you in the covenant of praise, we pray through our Lord. Amen.

We plough the fields and scatter
The good seed on the land,
But it is fed and watered
By God's almighty hand;
He sends the snow in winter,
The warmth to swell the grain,
The breezes and the sunshine,
And soft refreshing rain.

He only is the maker
Of all things near and far;
He paints the wayside flower,
He lights the evening star;
The winds and waves obey Him,
By Him the birds are fed;
Much more to us, His children,
He gives our daily bread.

We thank Thee, then O Father,
For all things bright and good;

The seedtime and the harvest,
Our lives, our health, our food;
No gifts have we to offer
For all Thy love imparts,
But that which Thou desirest,
Our humble, thankful hearts.

All good gifts around us
Are sent from Heaven above;
Then thank the Lord,
O thank the Lord
For all His Love. Amen.

Matthias Claudius, 1782

It becomes the just to be thankful, so we praise your name, O God, and magnify it with thanksgiving. Amen.

All things are Thine; no gift have we,
Lord of all gifts, to offer Thee;
And hence with grateful hearts today,
Thine own before Thy feet we lay. Amen.

John G. Whittier, 1873

Though we sit at the table, may we have the spirit of the one who serves. We ask through Christ, who was among us as one who served. Amen.

I offer thee—
Every flower that ever grew,
Every bird that ever flew,
Every wind that ever blew.
Good God!

Ancient Irish Prayer

Accept the praise of thankful hearts, our Father, we ask through Christ our Lord. Amen.

Thou who hast given so much to me
Give one thing more, a grateful heart,
For Christ's sake.

George Herbert
1593–1632

To you who brought streams out of rock,
who gives bread and meat to your people,
we return our thanks. Amen.

Thanks be to thee,
O Lord Jesus Christ,
For all the benefits
   which thou hast won for us;
For all the pains and insults
   which thou hast borne for us.
O most merciful Redeemer,
Friend and Brother,
May we know thee more clearly,
   love thee more dearly,
   and follow thee more nearly,
   for thine own sake. Amen.

Richard of Chichester
1197–1253

Heaven and earth praise you, O Lord. The sea and all things in it glorify you. We, the children of earth, come before you, bringing thanksgiving as our offering. Amen.

The things, good Lord, that we pray for,
give us grace to work for;
through Jesus Christ our Lord.

Thomas More
1478–1535

Dear God, thank you for your promise: "While the earth remains, seedtime and harvest, cold and heat, summer and winter, day and night will not cease." Amen.

(Genesis 8:22)

God, of your goodness give me yourself
for you are sufficient for me. I cannot prop-
erly ask anything less, to be worthy of you.
If I were to ask less, I should always be in
want. In you alone do I have all.

Julian of Norwich
1342–1443

Your loaves of mercy, Lord, increase according to our need. May we never doubt your love, nor fail in thanks for your faithfulness. Through Christ our Lord. Amen.

Lord, let Thy glory be my end,
Thy word my rule,
And then Thy will be done.

King Charles I
1600–1648

Our Father, may the praise of your children know no season, but be as constant as your love to us. Amen.

The Blessing of God
rest upon all those who have been kind to
     us,
have cared for us, have worked for us, have
     served us,
and have shared bread with us at this
     table.

Our merciful God,
reward all of them in your own way.
For yours is the glory and honor forever.
Amen.

*St. Cyril of the Coptic Orthodox Church,
Alexandria*, A.D. *412*

Put a new song in our mouths, most gracious God, the song of praise for all your benefits. Through Christ, we pray. Amen.

Lord of the harvest, hear
  thy needy servants cry;
Answer our faith's effectual prayer,
  And all our wants supply.

On thee we humbly wait,
  Our wants are in thy view:
the harvest truly, Lord, is great,
  the laborers are few.

Charles Wesley, 1707–1788

Deliver me, O God, from a slothful mind, from all lukewarmness and all dejection of spirit. I know these cannot but deaden my life to thee; mercifully free my heart from them, and give me a lively, zealous, active and cheerful spirit that I may vigorously perform whatever thou commandest and be ever ardent to obey in all things thy holy love.

John Wesley, 1703–1791

Thou art never weary, O Lord, of doing us good. Let us never be weary of doing thee service. But, as thou hast pleasure in the prosperity of thy servants, so let us take pleasure in the service of our Lord, and abound in thy work, and in thy love and praise evermore. O fill up all that is wanting, reform whatever is amiss in us, perfect the thing that concerneth us. Let the witness of thy pardoning love ever abide in all our hearts.

John Wesley, 1703–1791

Lord of heaven and earth and parent of us all, hear us as we offer thanks for the gift of bread. Amen.

As the sun doth daily rise,
brightening all the morning skies,
so to thee with one accord
lift we up our hearts, O Lord.

Day by day provide us food,
for from thee come all things good;
strength unto our souls afford
from thy living bread, O Lord.

Latin hymn;
translated by J. Masters;
adapted by Horatio Nelson, 1864

Almighty God, whose loving
hand hath given us all that we possess:
Grant us grace that we may honor thee
   with our substance,
remembering the account which we must
   one day give,
faithful stewards of thy bounty may be,
through Jesus Christ our Lord.

The Book of Common Prayer, 18th century

O God, our Father,
the foundation of all goodness,
Who has been gracious to us,
not only in the year that is past
but throughout all the years of our lives;
we give you thanks for your loving kindness
which has filled our days
and brought us to this time and place.

John Wesley, 1703–1791

Into thy hands, O Father and Lord, we commend our souls and bodies, our parents and our homes, friends and servants, neighbours and kindred, our benefactors and brethren departed, all folk rightly believing, and all who need thy pity and protection. Light us all with thy holy grace, and suffer us never to be separated from thee, O Lord in trinity, God everlasting.

Edmund Rich
1170–1240

Because your loving kindness is better than life, our lips will praise you, O God, and we will bless you as long as we live. Amen.

(Psalm 63:3)

Be present at our table, Lord,
Be here and everywhere adored;
Thy creatures bless, and grant that we
May feast in Paradise with thee.

John Wesley, 1703–1791

Power belongs to God; but also to you, our loving Lord, belongs loving-kindness and daily care for all your children. Our hearts are exalted that such a God is our God. Amen.

O Lord,
never suffer us to think
that we can stand by ourselves,
and not need thee.

John Donne
Seventeenth Century

In these days so perilous,
Lord, peace in mercy send us;
No God but thee can fight for us,
No God but thee defend us;
    Thou our only God and Savior.

Martin Luther
Sixteenth Century

Dearest Lord, teach me to be generous;
Teach me to serve thee as thou deservest;
To give and not to count the cost,
To fight and not to heed the wounds,
To toil and not to seek for rest,
To labour and not to seek reward,
Save that of knowing that I do thy will.

Ignatius of Loyola
Sixteenth Century

For a Mother-Daughter Banquet

Dear God, thank you for this joyous opportunity for rich fellowship with you and with one another.

Let all of us have the sense of wonder that children know and the steadfastness of character that belongs to true maternal hearts everywhere. From this happy occasion may we draw energy and strength for the tasks of this troubled generation. Show us how to combine a vision of a peaceful future with wisdom to solve the many problems of the present age. May we remember always our precious heritage as Christian mothers and daughters.

Bless this food to our bodies and this fellowship to our hearts. In Jesus name. Amen.

For a Father-Son Event

Dear heavenly Father, thank you for this opportunity for fathers and sons to meet together in happy fellowship under the auspices of our church home. Let each of us be aware that we are indeed Sons of God, our heavenly Father.

Help us to be better men and boys in future days because of the inspiration of this meeting. As we spend time together in fun and enjoying this food, may we realize anew the joys of living Christian lives. Help us to return a portion of our substance and ourselves to the work of your kingdom, serving you better as fathers and sons. Amen.

For a Church Christmas Breakfast

Our dear kind loving heavenly Father, on this special occasion in the time of Christmas, we come humbly to your throne of grace, asking for your loving blessing. We pray for a renewed understanding of our universal love and compassion. Grant that from this happy morning we may find vigor for the special errands of this season. Keep all of us and our absent dear ones in the light of your healing love. Bless this food to our bodies and this fellowship to our hearts. May we remember all year that Christmas is the reconciling of God and humanity through the coming of your son, Jesus Christ, in whose name we pray. Amen.

For a Sunday School Christmas Party

Dear God, at this happy season when we observe the birth of your Son, Jesus, hear our thanks for the many precious memories of Christmas in our homes and in this church. Grant us a special portion of your love as we meet now in Christian fellowship for joyous celebration. Let our outreach to others be expressed in the gifts we share from our hearts and from our hands. May the light of Christmas be seen in a mellowed glow of service that will permeate our lives in the coming year. Help us to accept fully the great gift of your son as the most precious heritage from the beloved Christmas season. Amen.

For a Women's Membership Coffee

Our loving Lord, thank you for the privilege of meeting together again as the fall season begins. Grant to each of us here today fresh energy for the tasks that lie ahead. May this be a year of rich fellowship with one another and with you. Give us guidance to do your will in our largest projects and in our smallest acts of devotion.

Bless this food to our bodies and this fellowship to our hearts. These mercies we ask in the precious name of Jesus Christ, our Lord and our Savior. Amen.